A Sacred Bond Broken

Daniel L. Walker, Sr.

Table of Content

Copyright   5-6

Dedication 7

Preface   8

Foreword 9

Personal Thoughts 10-11

Introduction 12-14

Prologue 15-20

Chapter 1: Who am I 21

Chapter 2: A Sacred Bond Broken 33

Chapter 3: H.E.L.P 56

Chapter 4: Silence 70

Chapter 5: Creative Hearts 82

Chapter 6: 1ne Dream 95

Chapter 7: Masterpiece 105

In Loving Memory 133-134

Afterword 135-136

Acknowledgements 137-139

Author Projects 140

Credits 141

Atlanta Division

An imprint of 9 Productions Group L.L.C

P.O. Box 2257

Loganville, Georgia 30052

9i9eproductiongroups@gmail.com

9PG Publishing and the distinctive logos is a registered trademark of 9 Productions Group L.L.C.

Library of Congress Number: 2014919567

The Library of Congress

U.S. Programs Law and Literature

101 Independence Avenue S.E.

Washington, D.C 20540-4283

The Library of Congress has cataloged the paperback edition as follows: Walker, Daniel 1972-

A Sacred Bond Broken/Daniel L. Walker-1st Ed.

Printed in the United States of America

10 9 8 7 6 5 4 3 2 1

Copyright © 1994, 2011, 2013, 2015 9 Productions Group L.L.C.

Introduction Copyright © 2013 Daniel L. Walker, Sr.

Foreword Copyright © 2014 Ka'Lysta A. Greene

Personal Thoughts Copyright © 2014 Brittney R. Smith

Personal Thoughts Copyright © 2014 Carla Dunlap

All rights reserved. This book contains material protected under International and Federal Copyright Laws and Treaties. Any unauthorized reprint or use of this material is prohibited. No part of this book may be reproduced or transmitted in any form or by any means, electronic or mechanical, including photocopying, recording or by any information storage and retrieval system without express written permission from the author/publisher.

ISBN: 10: 0692321411
ISBN-13: 978-0692321416

DEDICATION

This project is dedicated to my grandchildren Tateionna N. Warren and Jaliah Walden, I love you both very much……..God Bless

Preface

This book began in 2001, after the birth of my son Daniel L. Walker, Jr. At this time in my life I have been married to my wife Teirra Walker for about 3 years. Together we endured many tough times, but none more difficult than the passing of my mother Lula Mae Walker. In June 2001, our family clan would reunite for my mother's home going service.

I truly believed that day changed my life forever. I refused to be bothered with any of my siblings because of how they mistreated me as a child. I started to isolate myself from everyone, even my wife. One day after a huge argument with my wife, we both said hurtful things to hurt one another.

By September of 2003, I would leave for Los Angeles, California hoping for a better life. While sitting on Manhattan Beach, all I ever wanted was to be left alone so I could gather my thoughts. Believe it or not this is where my passion for writing would come in place once again.

Foreword

Ka'Lysta A. Greene

Daniel Walker has truly inspired me because he is a wonderful man and father. The way he treats my mother, is the way I want my future husband to treat me. The way he treats his children, is the way I want my children's father to treat them.

Daniel always makes me laugh, especially during tough times; we have a better relationship than my own father and I. He has taught me that I do not need a man to become a woman. I'm glad that I finally have a positive male role model in my life, he is an amazing person.

Ka'Lysta A. Greene is a 20 year old student from East Liverpool, Ohio majoring in Sports Medicine.

Personal Thoughts

My uncle Danny has always been a positive influence in my life. I have been living from house to house since the passing of my mother in 2012. Although I was faced with many obstacles, my uncle has always been there for me.

He encouraged me to continue to attend college, and to follow my dreams. When my uncle published his first book God's Rain: Poetry of Love, Life, and Family 1st Edition in 2014, it has showed me that anything is possible as long as you put your mind to it. His success showed me that it will not rain forever.

Brittney R. Smith

10/2014

Daniel and I have discussed the bias displayed toward him as a single father; they certainly differ from the ones faced by single mother. Daniel knows that he can't wallow in self pity; because he has children to finish raising, and will not be stopped by doors being slammed in his face.

It encourages me to see him get up after each knock down, becoming a widower, having limited resources, and not having a vehicle or the uncertainty about the future. The one thing I never saw waiver, was his faith in God. I am expecting to see many more spectacular things in the future from Daniel, and his family.

Carla Dunlap

10/2014

Introduction

Back Down Memory Lane

Welcome to the final installment of my book series titled *Overcoming Obstacles*, which tells many stories of my struggles. In life we face many challenges that sometimes can be for the good, or turn out to be very bad.

It doesn't matter who wins or who loses, but the most important aspect should be was a lesson learned. For those of you that read my debut novel *God's Rain*, may now have an understanding of the struggles, disappointments, and pain I faced in my life.

After five years of trying to put my life back together, over time I am still asked the same questions on how our family over came tragedy. At the same time I talk about my own struggles as a single father.

My life began in the humble beginnings of Midland, Pennsylvania, which being the youngest of seven children of Bennie and Lula Walker wasn't an easy task. In this large family we would sit back, and see how our mother dealt with so much mental and physical abuse.

After my father died in 1978 from throat cancer, this is when I would begin to experience Hell on earth. All my life I felt my mother was living with some sort of mental disorder, it wasn't until I was 14 years old when her behavior changed for the worst.

For instance, there were times that my mother would disappear for days, and I not know if she was dead or alive. By the age of 16, I would begin to live life as a homeless teenager on the streets of Pittsburgh, Pennsylvania.

As I began to get older many problems would seem to occur in my life. In 1996 I began dating Teirra Jones, who would later become my wife. We were married on May 23, 1998, and together we had 3 children Jaimie, Danyel, and Daniel. Our marriage was constantly tested with many obstacles, which included alcohol abuse and infidelity.

In 2001 my mother died, and this was when my passion for writing would begin to surface again. All I ever wanted was to tell a story that inspired someone, and make a difference in their life. In 2009, tragedy would strike our family like never before, with the passing of my wife. Later in 2012 our family would deal with the untimely passing of my sister Melissa A. Williams.

Many questions were asked if I could rise to the occasion, and raise my children as single father. All I ever wanted as a single parent was to make sure my children had a great childhood, even if their mother was no longer with us. In 2013, my life would forever change when I began writing a song called "God's Reign".

This song was a dedication to my wife who died in 2009. One day in 2012 I began taking a counseling session with a dear friend of mine who asked me to do a simple task.

This task would be a life changing experience because I was told to get a sheet of paper, and write down my thoughts of people who hurt me in life. So I did what was asked of me, and the birth of my first novel titled **God's Rain: Poetry of Love, Life, and Family** was created.

So as you read through this series I hope you get a chance to understand, and learn how I became the man I am today. This project is about facing life's challenges, and overcoming them by the grace of our Lord and Savior. I hope you all enjoy my short stories of overcoming obstacles.

Daniel L. Walker, Sr.

11/15/2013

Prologue
December 23, 2011

December 23, 2011

It's the holiday season, the sound of happiness and people laughing. I guess for me there isn't much happiness for in my life, except for walking through the hallway of the Allegheny County Courthouse in Pittsburgh, Pennsylvania. My spirits began to be lifted as I saw my daughter Jaimie being extremely well dressed. From a distance she looked so beautiful just like her mother.

As my children's father I have always taught them to dress professional at all times. Seeing my 18 year old daughter brought a smile to my face, she gave me the biggest hug. Then I looked into her eyes, and saw there were tears of pain in her eyes.

"So where is Tateionna", I asked? "She is with her father, but tomorrow we will be over to spend Christmas with you all", Jaimie replied. Walking down the hallway we can see the District Attorney walking toward us. "Hello Mr. Walker", he replied. "Mr. Walker we are going to have the homicide trial of your wife Teirra N. Walker today".

"You have to go to the witness room downstairs until we come, and get you" said the District Attorney. Just the thought of actually going through a homicide trial made me sick to my stomach.

As I walked through the door, all the attention was on me. Just imagine 6'7 black man dressed in a 3 piece suit. After I checked in with the receptionist I was told to have a seat. My heart was started pumping, and goose bumps began to form on my arms.

I began to ask myself if this was really it, can this nightmare be finally over. For over 2 years, all I ever wanted was to know the truth on what happen on January 18, 2009.

The sound of the door opening once again, all eyes are focus on who is coming into this room. It's Detective Wilson; he has the driver of the Port Authority bus that collided with the vehicle my wife was a passenger in. The bus driver sat next to me, for a minute I wondered if I should say anything to this guy.

So after 20 minutes passed I asked," hello how are you doing?" The bus driver just sat there with no reply. I glanced at the clock, I had less than 10 minutes before the homicide trial would begin to start. So this time, I turned and extended my hand in friendship. "My name is Daniel Walker, my wife was Teirra Walker", and the bus driver turned said,"are you talking to me?" "Yes sir I am".

"Well first off, I am so sorry about your wife", said the bus driver. "I can only begin to imagine what you are going through". "Did you have any kids together", he relied? "Yes, we had 3 kids".

I can see his eyes had tears forming, which told me this man had a heart. "You know Mr. Walker, I have had the hardest time trying to come to terms that someone died", said the bus driver. "That vehicle was going so fast compared to all the other vehicles on the Homestead Grays Bridge".

"I could see your wife as the car was approaching my way. Our eyes connected with each other before the collision", said the bus driver. Something told me to turn around, and the whole room was focused on our conversation. There was an older African American woman sitting across from us, she came over to me, and said" your wife was the lady from the bus accident"." God will see you through all of this madness, and great things will come into your life".

For a moment I thought this lady was crazy, but I remember a conversation with my sister, she told me when this is over God will give you the answers you have been seeking.

With the sound of the door opening there was the District Attorney standing there to take us up to the courtroom. So as the trial began, the courtroom was packed with many people, and I glimpsed over to the accused for one brief moment. Jaimie came over, and for once I felt complete.

Having my daughter there was a sense of closure for me. I remember promising to all 3 of my kids I would get them answers on what happened to their mother.

If I had to walk through the gates of Hell bare foot I would give them some answers. So together Jaimie and I sat through every testimony, and even when they played the video of the bus accident. So the judge asked the accused to stand before her peers in the courtroom. Jaimie and I both sat there just stunned that this is actually occurring, we both held our head down with tears in our eyes.

The judge told the accused she was found not guilty. Jaimie got up and walked out the courtroom, for me it was a relief. I did not care if she was found guilty or innocent. Out in the hallway Jaimie was crying, but she had that family support.

Many victims of violent crimes are stuck to pick up the pieces all by themselves. Jaimie had her grandmother, aunts, uncles, and her father. I told Jaimie not to worry because now we can live knowing the truth.

Here I am in the cold outside the courthouse watching Teirra's family walk to their cars. One thing I can count on is when it came to Teirra's family no matter how bad things seemed their faith is what made them such a strong family.

On December 26, 2011, there was the sound of thawing ice falling on my porch. I sat in my living room the day after Christmas, still in disbelief. However, my focus was now my children Danyel and Daniel Jr.

No matter how family members felt, my primary goal is to make sure they would grow up living a happy life. So with that being said, we would leave Washington, Pennsylvania for Atlanta, Georgia. I could no longer live in a place that took everything I once loved.

One thing I learn from this experience is January 18, 2009 was my wife's choice to leave. No matter how tragic her life may have ended there is still hope for our legacy to continue to thrive.

Chapter 1

Who Am I

Just 1 Hug

All I ever needed is just 1 hug. Just a feeling that there is a sense of love, imagine being on top of the world later to find out now the world is on top of you. What more can a man do?

Just 1 hug is all I need. Is that too much to ask? Why is this sense of emotion so complicated? At times I might want to cry, but can I just have one before I die. Maybe this is why I had so many one night stands. All I wanted was a sincere hug.

Just one there is no other reason, maybe this is why none of them made it through this season. I promise you that one person that gives me that 1 hug of sincere love will become my wife.

All I ever wanted was that ingredient that is so small, but has manifested into a hopeless disease. All I ever wanted mama was just 1sincere hug to make me feel loved. We get tired of being a lonesome dove. This road we call life can be rough, especially now because I am no longer tough.

Spoken Words from the Streets

Last night I had this dream about heaven, maybe some things aren't what they truly seem, I use to live my life based on the C.R.E.A.M. Deep down inside no one knows the day or the hour because at the end of the day our heavenly father has the power.

So ask yourself where do we begin, how many will lose their souls because of sin? This poem is dedicated to my mother because without your hard up bringing who knows where I might be. I thank you for your constant prayers. Somewhere along the lines I know each one of those prayer saves me.

I remember mama's favorite song" Amazing Grace" my favorite line is I was lost, but now I'm found. As we struggle just know these chains are no longer bound. My focus is being around those that are spiritually healthy. Instead of losing my soul from those whose main focus is being wealthy.

Reminisce

Go ahead my father drop your tears, may I tell your peers about your long lost daughter that you miss. In the town of "Leopards "because of rumors you were dissed. For my protection I chose a knife instead of a gun, but S. C. can you look after my son?

  A birthday kiss that set a memory a drift, to us it was missed. Life's choices would incite unfamiliar voices. Mama's constant prayers from afar would be heard. Who are you praying for? "My family", she replied. Many nights God spared my life. Move two steps to the left as the heat from a gunman's bullet almost left me unconscious to meet death.

  Stayed up half the night as love put me through changes, knowing our house was not a home. Tired of being alone the streets she would roam. Enter alcohol with a mixture of infidelity, what do you have? Complete hell. Sad faces distant places life's token. Can a man be broken?

  One story 2 versions, which one is false, which one is fact. To the world you have already faded to black. Asking God for so much, was this my empty prayers. Pain be 4 pleasure, finally has true love to treasure at my own measures. Haters going to hate, Takers going to take.

Who am I

In the jungles I am hunted like a thief in the night. There were times many may have feared me because of my appearance. I know you heard my cries for help, but it was your decision to ignore me.

My hands may feel tied, my burden you will bear. To your despair I always wondered if you would be there. Yet I have asked the question who are you? From the start I wiped your tears when you were sad, and carried you when you were weak, but the question still remain who do you seek?

Since I have you in my life, I can climb any mountain to the highest peak. Yet I told you, I will never leave you or forsake you, but you still don't know me. In the rain all things still remain the same. Maybe the walls will tumble, and the sun may refuse to shine. After all our hard work, and achievements you still decide to keep my existence confined.

I thought I was the Omega and the Alpha, or the king of kings. Every Sunday morning it's about my glory that we sing. I have been with you since the terrors of Ghana, and the tragedies of New York.

I have roamed the earth for centuries, looking for those chosen ones to carry on my work. If you noticed on the beach, when you needed me I was there, my proof was the set of foot print I left for you to see.

Even though you had heartaches and pain, or when you're loved ones have passed on to eternal life I was still there. During your incarcerations I was there, but why do you still decide to deny me. I am your Heavenly Father, and your savior Jesus Christ.

Who am I pt.2

A leopard never changes his spots; he rearranges them, that's what they use to say about me. Was there truly another chapter to this life? Believe it or not, I never knew how to love you even though we stood before God while accepting a wife.

Each day that goes by I miss you, someone said that because of my mistakes that this marriage is through. So now in 2015, I lay here all alone hoping for a brighter future, but my dreams constantly have me reliving the past. Let me reminisce on how our life use to be, was it really that bad, that's what I constantly ask?

Was these one night stand really worth it all? Many people felt that I never rally deserved your love, maybe this is true. After all the countless women, and Saturday night fights was I to blame for your death?

Some of you judged me based on assumptions, did you ever consider that I did have a broken heart. Maybe your focus was tearing it apart, because she had someone who truly cared.

It's funny how your own siblings thought my focus was spending Teirra's money. No matter if I lived my life in sin, I was still her husband left to raise 3 kids.

For so many years I still fought back my tears, and somehow I was able to be strong. Deep down inside my inner strength was being chipped away, so it was at that moment when I prayed. So who am I?

I dealt with my issues and addictions, but each day I've learned that I was surrounded by so many unhealthy friends and family. No matter what obstacles I faced, it feels good to know that have the ability to tell you all that I finally know who I am.

Think about U

Let me take a little time to tell you all how my life use to be. At one time I thought it was all about me. All I do is think about you; just imagine how life could be if family put love first. All my life I thought I was cursed because of my father's sins.

All I do is think about you; ever since that hurtful phone conversation my life has never been the same. It kills me that the only way for me to communicate with you would be through this poem. For once, take time to think how exciting life would be if you would know this dream I have is not just for me.

Each night I drop a tear, so maybe this love I have for you will stay. It's crazy how an overnight sensation changed my life. Now all of your hurtful remarks are done out of spite.

All I do is think about all 6 of my siblings. I can finally say there is happiness in my life as it seems. After all my struggles, and pain I can actually say I am living my dream. Each day I live, I will always love you because all I do is think about you.

Let the Tears from Heaven Flow

Will these tears of sorrow bring hope for a better tomorrow? Just let the tears from heaven flow. My pain brought *God's Rain*, which helped me wipe away my tears for years. I rise and fall, yet through it all it's your holy name we call.

Let the tears from heaven flow, loves broken heart that has been torn nearly apart. The American Dream, is all than just a heartbeat away, but now it's been destroyed, what more to do but pray.

My finest day is still unknown, no place to truly call my own. Let the tears from heaven flow, many nights my heart still grieves. Lord do you hear my plea, when you call me home I will finally be free.

Lonely

Here I am consumed in the dark room of pain. Sometimes my heart may bleed with shame. At times I may still feel sad. As I look to my right, what must this be that has held me down for so long? Maybe it's those lonely love songs.

True my life is still sad and weary, but the pain I try to hide still hurts severely. The world knows at times I did you wrong. So go ahead and laugh, as I soak in this pain. Let me ask you, what did you gained from this lonely heart of sadness?

So let me give you a round of applause, because you all have succeeded in bringing me misery. For years I have been filled with hate. When a nephew needed help you turned your back. When a niece needed support she was told to get your life on track.

The love of family, can't you feel the sensation, until another creation of life. As her baby cries, you ignored her maybe she can't feed a child because she is poor. Let me be the next to leave since my heart still greaves. My world has fallen apart maybe because of a broken heart.

It's hard when your life is scrambled in pieces. My heart cries for my nieces. I have been on this road all alone with no home. Is there a place filled with love?

Maybe the heavens above you lonesome dove. So come fly with me so he can prepare our place. Trust me this world is no place to be. We need a place that is carefree, a place of prosperity, and a place just for you and me, so come take me away as I am dressed in white.

I am clean and pure as a white knight. Don't cry, because I am in a better place, and no longer will I live Hell on earth. Now all the pain can cease, because I have found a place called peace.

Chapter 2

A Sacred Bond Broken

Broken Hearts, Shattered Dreams

Last night I had a dream that all things were still the same. We sang and danced in perfect harmony, not having to worry about the negative aspects of the world to gain.

There were many sounds of laughter, but was it just a dream, or was it reality. Our lives are now like a shattered mirror, all broken up with so many missing pieces. Still forced to live with all this hurt, and pain that life has to offer, one may ask themselves where do I turn?

Can I go to that relative that only wants to be bothered when it is convenient for them? Maybe I can offer you my wealth, because the color of green is all that's seen.

As I lay on the floor with my eyes soaked from tears of sorrow. I know this is where my strength lies; maybe time will get better tomorrow. All I have now are many memories. Many nights our children called your name, wishing that all we went through was just a dream, but in reality, society reminds us of that fateful day so it seems.

Written 02/02/2009

After the Rain

After the rain came life was still not the same. Some wanted to play games, even I needed a change. Flowers no longer bloomed; my sanctuary was still my room. God hid my tears from my peers, and promised me there wouldn't be any more fears. My world is better because you came in time. God took away the rain, and replaced it with sunshine.

I truly believed no weapon formed against me shall prosper. Just know that life now has so much to offer. As I think about America's youth maybe we should speak the truth. Finally, there a place called peace were all this drama has ceased.

Thank God I am no longer followed by dark clouds. At times I may roam these streets like a thief in the night. Maybe try building a fortress for protection, but life still brings another rejection. I am a quiet storm in a world of thunder. Who refuse to let man put us under?

Abuse

As a child cries so helplessly inside because her mental scars may tell a story, at night she prays to God, so this bad dream may end. To the world she is speechless because of her step-father's daily sins.

There isn't a day that goes by, as she is still filled with pain. At night she cries to God, and ask what did I truly gain? Who is to blame?

Can my step-father really make a change; my life is constantly filled with pain. Her art becomes her escape, because she was raped at age eight. She cries for help through her art, which explains the malice this child had in her heart.

Is God truly the expression for pain or passion, when I am with you I am lost for words. My life seems to be helpless and hopeless because what is real can it be possible with God on my side.

How can someone be so forgiving, which makes my life not worth living? The very sight of him makes my skin crawl because of his constant penetration that was extremely raw. Many nights she cries to be released from this hell.

How can I help those that were constantly abused? As we sleep, a helpless child cries. As we pray, another child dies.

Can we create a world that doesn't have a sense of fear? Together we are united to cry happy tears. Let us fight for justice against child abuse, and save those who are constantly preyed upon.

A Little White Line

Just a little white line that's all it is, I began to tell myself. Maybe just one hit won't hurt. Baby girl took it out of her purse to be evenly disbursed. Watch it be separated into 3 lines. My heart gets to racing, loud music, many strange faces, and unknown places.

I take one sniff and it burns like hell. Lord knows if I get caught I could end up in jail. My nose starts to drip, in a room filled with tricks. My heart gets to racing, loud music, many strange faces, and unknown places.

My world is in a daze, now they wanna light and blaze. Can't do it vision is a little hazy. My homeboy in the corner passed out with 2 females; got me over here sweating now I am feeling crazy.

For one night of fun it felt like I was losing life. My kids can't take another tragedy knowing that I just lost my wife. I feel so lost, can't to believe I was willing to pay the major cost. Thank God I didn't do any time. All this occurred just because of one hit of these mysterious white lines.

Written 08/20/2010

A Sacred Bond Broken

Respect what God has given you, that's what everyone use to tell me. True it was my decision to break this circle. Your family use to say it would never work because we are unequally yoked. Maybe they had blind eyes and deaf ears, because for years we lived a double life. My focus was trying to please my wife.

Remember there are 2 sides to this story, but the other half isn't here to tell her side. At times I was mistreated, which explains why I cheated. True I left my family for 2 years, but did you ever consider that I had my own mental scars. This little town treated us like modern day stars; it was you who focused more on local bars.

People will claim to love you while smiling in your face, even when they swear to live their life by the bible. At times I felt we really weren't family, but more of a personal rival. Deep down inside I know my success made you feel distasteful. After all the personal attacks including identity theft, which left my love for you feeling disgraceful.

I promise myself not to ever leave with hate, but how can I forget all the bad you wished for me. Your right all I cared about are my two kids, especially after all the spiteful things you did. Some people will only support you when it's beneficial.

I remember when you said my family was useless, and they all had issues. True those remarks did hurt, but Karma is revengeful so now it's your turn to grab a tissue.

So this sacred bond was broken, but it was still fixable. Maybe we were afraid to let go because we could no longer put on a show.

The only thing that is left after your tragic death is our kids. Yes, our kids? It seems like everyone who came by had smiling faces. Deep down inside, none of your promises were even close to being true.

So now it's 2015, my kids are much older and wiser, maybe this is why we have chosen to give you the cold shoulder. All I can do is wish the best for their lives. In the beginning, this family's platform was built on love. It was me that decided to break this sacred bond, by finally choosing to move on.

Back in the Day

I remember the times we shared, even though we had more good days than bad. As I walked on Memory Lane the thoughts of you made me sad. Damn how I wish those days would come back again.

From every prayer, and every sin I wonder where we should begin. From our very own bottle of Dom Perignon, to our Four Seasons Hotel Suite. Many nights you cried from the pain you consumed. I can remember Manhattan Beach, and the million dollar house made of glass. All the things we would buy with his monetary stash.

Even though the world seemed like they didn't want us together. So we made love just to make our bad times seem better. Is it true, I was not your only lover? As I walked through your house there were so many pictures of this brotha. We drank a bottle of Gin, then you confessed to me about your husband.

As we laid on this bed fully undressed. I just thought about how you are so blessed. This man would have given you the world if he could. Well since we are here with true confessions, can I tell you about my life? The person I call from time to time is more than just a friend, she is my wife.

As I looked in your eyes I couldn't help, but to fall in love. When we first met I thought this was a gift from the heavens above. We both claimed that both of our relationships were filled with pain. Somehow you refuse to leave because of your spouse's financial gain.

Now you tell me that you are carrying my child. You need to tell your husband because your body will change in a while. Your reply, what about your wife? How is she going to feel about our new life?

Bad Habits

I've given so much in the past, but it seems that wasn't enough. You know men do have feelings too, I would've walked through the gates of Hell just to make a point. Why do I have to prove myself to somebody just to be considered worthy? I remember when you told me that there wouldn't be a woman to except me with my faults.

That was your biggest mistake because you sent me to the streets. Maybe I was wrong, because my focus is supposed to be you, but what is a man like me to do? It happened with a single kiss from too much Vodka. Deep inside we knew this wasn't right, but what can really happen in just one night. When I get home there will be another fight because it's five in the morning.

Somehow I go to shake this bad habit, but she made me feel like a man. I wish my wife could really understand that she lead me into this older woman's hand. She tells me what I love to hear, and even treats me with respect. A wife knows her husband from head to toe, but now I am starting to change. This affair is getting out of range, with trips out of town. So it's the Fourth of July 2003, we take it to a whole new level. My sister tells me that I will burn in hell along with that devil.

As I arrive home things are not the same, as I head upstairs, on the left night stand lays an open condom wrapper. I keep my composure, since my wife just confirmed that I wasn't the only one cheating. Maybe this relationship wasn't meant to be, since we both have our scars? Is this one of her games? Who is really the blame? Somehow I got to explain myself, because we both need help.

What about our kids, after all the spiteful things we both did? Which one of us was going to finally become an adult? I thought this marriage would prosper, but this infidelity has nothing to offer. One day my mistress decided to leave when she told me she already had a husband. Her statement was something I refuse to believe, but she exposed my weakness because after all I am still a man.

9 of Swords: A God's Rain Prequel

9 of Swords: Part 1

For the first time in my life I felt hopeless, imagine being with someone for over 12 years, and then one day she is gone forever. At one moment in my life I felt ashamed; my mother spent her whole life teaching me to say no to drugs. It's true that Teirra Walker and I had an unhealthy marriage; the good did outweigh the bad.

Deep down inside I was screaming for help, but my pride kept me silent. Never in my wildest dreams did I ever think that one person could mean so much to me, but when she left, I felt as if my life didn't really matter. No one will ever understand how much I was hurting. I still wish I could have all those bad moments back, just so I can make it right. It's scary how over the counter sedatives can almost destroy your life?

God you promised that you will never leave me, or forsake me and this statement is so true. When Satan released his legions of demons to destroy me, God you were there to protect me and set me free. "Many asked me how I was able to quit", my reply **God's Rain.**

Imagine being so high, that you have no clue what road you're on. As I sat on my porch in the still of the night, it was then that I felt God's comfort in the rain. We all dream of being on top of the world, but how would we react when the world is on top of you. Think about it!!!

9 of Swords: Part 2

Lord can you please help me to get some sleep, that's what I kept telling myself. True my situation has changed, maybe it was my lack of awareness that made me want to stay. My family kept telling me something has to change because my attitude is a little out of range.

A distant dark place, that promised to set me free. It came to me in a demonic figure, maybe this will set me free. Many dreams would turn into daily plea for help. Was I this mentally scarred prisoner in jail, my heartfelt broken and on a one way trip to a place called Hell? My own mother couldn't even understand, maybe this is why she refused to lend a helping hand.

Her reply," this is the road you chose for your life, I can't believe my own son claims he is ready to take a wife". My life was at a place of no return, it was guaranteed that my soul was destined to burn. When I closed my eye all I seen was this place of pain, which lead me to believe that I had gone insane.

With all this hurt and pain that continued to haunt me, can you at least just let me be? It's crazy how these pills has become my daily plea, true my life felt useless since the passing of "Tee". I now know this new lifestyle isn't right, but this is the road I chose all I have to do is just keep this addiction out of sight.

After mixing alcohol with sedatives then she came my savior, who can this be? Here I am standing on a subway headed on a one way trip to Hell. How can I count on you to save our legacy, when all your tears are being drained away in these mysterious pills?

To my right was a young figure that use to be my own wife, but as I looked to my left there was the Angel of Death. As a tear drops hit my face, Lord can you give me my own personal space. Many nights I wished this was a bad dream; it's so true that I didn't give you all my love. Maybe I should have continued to fill my body with these drugs, since this world refuse to show me any love.

Think about your kids, how would they cope, the only thing living for is hope. So from 2009-2011, my life was filled with societies modern day dope. Now that I am left in this world still going through it, there were times I wish I could have called your phone. So in 2013 I'm living this life all alone.

Some days are better than most, hoping that this was just a bad dream. My love for my wife did run deep. You know the good did outweigh the bad, which made me kind of sad because my life was once surrounded by alcohol and sedatives.

Many nights I cried for these bad dreams to come to an end. Most of the time all I thought about was sin. Here I stood facing many doors, door number 1 wanted to take my son.

Door numbers 2 refuse to let me make it through. There was door 3, which gave me a vision of how terrible my life could be. It's crazy how one phone call to a true friend, who introduced me to the Lord, which is how I overcame my own curse of the 9 of Swords.

So to those who had questions, yes my name is Daniel L. Walker. My wife was Teirra N. Walker, who died on the Homestead Grays Bridge in Pittsburgh, Pennsylvania. However, as a member of her family we refuse to let January 18, 2009 solidity our legacy. From her ashes we will continue to rise with each and every occasion.

I may have fallen victim to Satan, and his demons while grieving and being weak. Thank God for giving me the ability to tell this story to the world.

Based on a true story written 03/13/13

Untitled

As she rushes home and runs up the stairs, the sound of my sister's cries made me aware. Mother would force herself into her room." Oh my God! What happen to your face?" With her clothes torn to shreds, her favorite white shirt was now red. " He forced himself on me" she would cry.

The touch of his hands made me want to die. I screamed "why!" Just think this happen because of one simple hi. I slowly open the door with mother holding her so tight, maybe she will be alright. Her scars were visible because her skin complexion is extremely light.

Soon mother said "she was the blame". "Is this another one of your games", Mother asked ? It was one of your friends I tried to tame. You blame me for being late, said I acted like I was on a date. My body he would rape. Now I am filled with hate.

I found my sister in her room filled with tears. Mama's boyfriend has been touching me for years. The sound of his voice still brings fears. I have been afraid to tell my peers.

Many nights I heard her get sick. He treated her like his trick. Because of his sick dick, her body would begin to change. He laughed as this was a game. He already had her tamed. Her virginity he would claim.

She would cry mother how could you let this be; now I am pregnant and living with H.I.V. I just wanted him to die, as I cried. Mother thought this was my lie. What did I do that was so wrong? I can only take this pressure for only so long.

Got to love my mother as she continues to live her life in sin, I prayed that this night mare would soon end. Need to focus more on my health and my baby. I need to getaway don't feel loved anymore, especially from this lady.

I Got 2 Getaway

Sometimes I got to get away, so tire of systematic rules. So you claim to be my friend, then you try to tell me what to do. Tired of lies because last I checked this is my personal life, and I don't live it for you.

I got 2 get away, that what I keep telling myself. Time to focus on me and no one else, life is too short to be concerned about someone so simple minded. It's crazy how one night of bad choices can change your life forever.

I spent these past 5 years hiding from those that had questions. So as the media continues to write their lies, just know that I will no longer run and hide.

There you all go continuing to focus on small issues, but I will be forever hurt so there is no need to try to grab me a tissue. Is there such a place where I can escape, can I find a true friend that really wants to be around? Just be true to whom to you are instead of trying to stomp my legacy into the ground.

I got 2 getaway; maybe family will understand that there were so many problems that use to bother me. One time in my life I found true love, but money is all she ever thought of. I got 2 getaway, so can we make it from day to day? Even today there is no peace since my peer do not pray.

Sexual Thoughts

Funny how time flies when you're in the heat of passion. I guess the title of this song couldn't have said it better. Maybe I can send my love for you in this letter. ***Would you mind*** if we grinded from time to time. Yet I might want to ***go deep*** when you're ***moist.*** I love the high pitch from your voice. Let me ***throb*** before I explode inside.

Guaranteed it will make you feel really good. Can we go from front to back because time is against us, and it's almost time to go. We can do this all night, and even make our own version of ***24 Play***. The next day we can do this again every thought of you get me ***so excited***. I have many plans, but as long as it involves you I will be delighted. Trust me there isn't ***nothing*** I wouldn't do to be with you.

I love it when you are in ***control;*** this is more than just a sexual thought. Imagine how great this experience can be because my love for you will never stop. Your last message you kept asking me ***where are you now***. Just relax because I do ***miss you much,*** since this was just a mere thought. We need to ***wait a while*** until marriage because our focus is abstinence.

Inner City Blues

My son this world is so cold, granted there are some things you don't really know because you are only thirteen years old. Turn that frown into a smile. Life is about more than just material things.

Ask yourself who are really pleasing; still many of our brothas have died because of the triggers their squeezing. Our world's main focus is still race, your grandmother use to tell me that they would not stock an album cover with a black face. My son everybody thinks were lost, so many family members have paid the ultimate cost.

Remember these daily struggles because they are life's lessons. Many nights we cried, it's true we all hurt, especially that fateful night when your mother died. The sky is still the limit there are so many things we can do. Just know that this is our daily struggles, and our own version of "Inner City Blues".

Dedicated to my son "Daniel L. Walker, Jr."

Written June 29, 2014

This life here on earth is temporary, so make each moment mean something.

Love always and forever

Dad

When I Gave My Life 2 U

Just let me be that's what I keep telling myself. I know there were hearts that I stole even when my reaction was stone cold. There was a time when I said I needed you, but now my feet is still on solid ground.

T.F. you really hurt me even tried to take and deceive me, but look who's sorry now. You had a way of making people feel so sorry. No matter how harsh your insults were I knew with Christ there wasn't a mountain that I couldn't climb. All that was gained is shame. Then it happened, a change for me that I refuse to lose.

Standing at my left were my kids, which showed me to lead by example. Here we are standing at this alter confessing by tongue that we believed when he gave the world his only son.

Here we are filled with hugs and tears; no longer will I have fears. My focus is now to give God his time, and to take time to make a difference in someone's life. After all I been through I still remember that day I gave my life to you.

Chapter 3

H.E.L.P.
(Heal Each Less Fortunate Person)

2nd Chance

So the Lord wiped my tears. Now go ahead and tell your peers. So I chose to use my pen, and talk about my sins. So I got this second chance, so excited makes me wanna dance. I know this blessing won't be easy.

First you need to know that this love comes from heaven above. Just a word of caution, you need to be careful of who and what you trust. The world knows your weakness is lust. Trust me Satan will temp you with temptation.

Be prepared at all times, especially from this generation. No matter the challenge keep the faith. God will give you the space. No longer will I be afraid. No more lonely cries be encouraged and testify.

So I got my 2nd chance just want to tell the world in advance. Since I got a new life, how about another wife, I promise this time I will be nice. So I got my 2nd chance maybe I should give her a new romance.

This time we should take things slow, or go with the flow. Many won't understand what I mean by second chance. Maybe you might not be on my level, or might be on the same playground with the devil. Trust me it's not a fun place to be. I use to play there. Nobody cares to share. All the games are not played fair. So think twice if you want to keep your life.

Lyric

What I admired first is the way you flow. Your charisma made me feel this wasn't for show. We both have a passion for creative arts. Just add pen to this paper to tell our story of love, which captured my heart.

As we enter this room secluded in silence, it was then that our hearts began to make a move. Just close your eyes, and imagine a distant place that didn't care about our race. The only sound that can be heard is the drip from faucet to pan. Let me explain about me she replied. I write based off of my life and the struggles from peers.

This is why my eyes flow like I'm being baptized in the Red Sea. I began to express my testimony of my life, how one single night end my marriage to my wife. So we both write about pain, but what we were able to create was a blessing that will never be the same.

Keep the Faith

When all you ever wanted was just one chance, ask yourself is it possible to have more than just a glance. I know through life we have our daily struggles, but can we achieve that one dream before they throw dirt in my face with the shovel.

So no matter the hurt or the pain, you got to keep the faith. Peace is there such a place; maybe this dream is no longer worth wait. With ignorance to my right, and hate on my left make your choices before you face the Angel of Death.

As the world drops a tears because my legacy is all they will have left. As I ask my Lord to set me free, too much pressure from this world why can't they just let me be? So I will keep the faith, because this world still wants to judge by race.

So I now know that you care, yes my father you will be there when my nights are lonely. Many nights these bridges connected to my troubled waters. Even my own family didn't want to be bothered. So God lift me up, and show me you care. At times this life of mine can be a little unfair.

That's why through my doubts and frustrations I know you will be there. I know at times we struggle with sin, but a single touch from your hands will make it all end. So let me keep the faith, as I show the world my confidence will win out. Acknowledgement and respect of my art is what this is all about.

Maybe

Maybe we can live as one. Each day I thank God for my son. I refuse to let him live life by the laws of a gun. Maybe we can live this dream in peace, because in reality all good times has ceased. Try living for tomorrow instead of drowning in your tears of sorrow.

Maybe there is still hope for our broken families. Some wonder why there are constant tears in little Johnny's eyes. Could it be his daddy is long gone from a place called home? Maybe real fathers are locked away in jail, now there only sense of freedom will be hell. As my baby girl screams don't take daddy, now it's her pimp that she calls daddy.

Maybe I can send a prayer to Minolta, true she knows how to live and die in a city called Angel. Her past sins are the reasons she lives her life in the state's shackles. Maybe this poem can inspire the youth, some refuse to hear the truth. I have hope for the boy down the street, whose life has no peace.

Maybe it's true I do have sad eyes, because of childhood pain I tried to hide. Was I the one consumed with hate, because of a displaced case? My art has replaced malice in my heart. Maybe just maybe I have conquered my unsettled fears. Now in the year 2014, I still at night have crying tears.

One day I will give all my hard work to Danyel, because she is my world. True she is daddy's little girl. I just want your life to be simply alright, and happiness to last for more than just one night.

4 Seasons of Love

I'm in the city where the world doesn't know my name. To some they might want to point fingers, and say I am to blame. Its true my past sins may have made me feel guilty. I have dealt with your assumptions and extra added garbage, which at times makes me feel filthy.

So go ahead and defame my name with shame. Guess what I am still a major player in this game? So run along and tell your peers, that I know longer live my life in fear. Once again I call these streets my home. I can make you an offer that you can't refuse just like Michael Corleone.

Maybe I still got this sense of power, but it may cease at any given hour. Something has changed, there is no more fun carry this gun. I may have been forgiven by the Lord above, but ask yourself do these street still wanna show me any love?

In the streets, forgiveness begins and ends when your body no longer has breath, because you just met the Angel of Death. What happens when that so called lifelong friend stands before me as he watches you die? What scared me the most is when he removed his dark sunglasses, and revealed demonic eyes. Your biggest sin is that you trusted everyone even your best friend.

Will U Be There

To the world you sing out loud to create the largest crowd, but let me ask you this question. Will you be there? When I am hunted down like a thief in the night, even though some of the things I did wasn't quite right. Even when the media looks for a negative reaction it's my own story that has attraction.

Will you be there, when I am locked away for being educated and black? It's my appearance that is constantly attacked. Will you be there because I actually care? Will you fight against injustice that threatens our nation?

Will you be there when I'm searching out for angels just trying to find some peace? This battle we have against the police will it ever cease, or is this just the beginning for many wars, that the media will adore.

Music

We have been together for such a longtime, from the sound of your beat to the spoken words of a certain song. You have been in my family for generations; with this blessing we all knew there could be no wrong. From the Clarinet, Saxophone, Bass Drum, Trombone, Piano, and Electric Guitar, all has been a blessing from above.

The sound of music we hear, knowing that this was all made from love. The harmony of love is the most important, even though today it can be filled with hate. One person can change the world, so let's focus on more positive music that we create. Let your spirit be free.

Try this "C" chord got to stay on key. A sweet melody without a song, bring the joys of my heart. Maybe it was fragile as glass. Kicked around like yesterday's trash.

Use the beat of a perfect harmony to write a lyric of pain. To the world what you gain is the art of creativity. The world is left shocked because of your ability. The sweet sound of music; take my hand as we dance to many distant notes. I open with love, as my favorite white dove.

Maybe this talent was meant to be from you to me. With various notes all the world has is a sense of hope. Let us take a chance with this romance. As we listen to the quite storm can I have another slow dance?

H.E.L.P (Heal Every Less Fortunate Person)

Some of you think I'm crazy; maybe you're just mentally lazy. I have been on the run all my life from fear. Now that these chains have been released, my tears has ceased. This world is in turmoil. Our babies need discipline and guidance instead of incarceration.

Are we to blame for their failures, when there is lack of education. How can we be a strong nation when there are so many babies we still can't feed? Why is there still homelessness on the streets?

When will a war torn third world country finally have peace? Maybe one day this madness will cease. Did man reach his destination, but God still has no limitation. His work is still the mighty creation. As the world cries for help, so much pain and disbelief is still felt. Even when we try to stand tall, and at a weak moments it's his name we call.

I know I will make it through the night, since my faith has made this new life out of sight. I can cross that river, and make through to the other side. God's hand has guided me so this journey will be a smooth ride.

Blind Eyes, Deaf Ears

Blind eyes, deaf ears how many years should we see this pain that has been brought from society. It's true our leaders have deaf ears to some of their peers, which has left our country in tears.

So are you blinded by the truth? Everything I touch was dark with a sense of danger. So many lonely nights I was consumed in my bedroom. Hatred was my best friend, and smiles turned in to anger.

Maybe there is a sense of hope, as our nation copes with change. Why do we live on deaf ears, because there are no cheers for the poor? Are we too blind to feed the homeless, or are we too blind to help those who cannot read.

As we write what do we recite? When we create, is it too late to put hope on the blind and deaf ears. So run along, and tell our peers as we drown our sorrows in tears.

No Doubt

I still have those visions of achieving the American Dream. Many nights I cried because my dreams quickly have turned into nightmares as it seems. As the wind may blow my way, I still find time to pray. I still have those sudden fears that brought me many tears from all my peers.

No doubt I still don't know what this is all about. I wonder when I die will I see heaven. Then again my biggest sin happened when I was bout eleven. Who can you trust, especially when my world is filled with lust? Sometimes I just want to give everything away, sad looks from my kids gave me the inspiration to wanna stay.

No doubt this did hurt, even at times I feel like I am still cursed. So much pain for one man to endure, same shit different day this I know for sure. Some say man is not happy until he dies. The last thing I want to do is put tears of sadness in my kids' eyes. No doubt we are living in our final days. Let's just hope we can make it in our very own special way.

Change

In the still of the night I try to keep out of sight. The lifestyle I live isn't quite so right. As I run from house to house, what I leave behind is shattered glass and infamous footprints. I have hurt many people in my past.

Maybe I should repent; my old life has to end. Instead of roaming the streets at night I now move during the day. Every morning I drop to my knees and pray. The cops now know me by name, some refuse to believe I am no longer in the game.

My friends felt betrayed because now I have made it. It's true I have made a change, don't care if I am to blame. Then one late night I heard a knock at the door. Who could this be that wants to see me?

As I open the door a single shot is fired. The shot strikes me in the chest. Now I lay on the floor dropping a tear from the corner of my eyes, and gasping for air as I am about to meet death.

Chapter 4

Silence

We've had Enough

This world we live in is no longer safe. Fear lurks around every corner, maybe because of race. Father God can you save this place, or are we better off catching a legal case. I know there maybe some things that I don't truly understand. Maybe this is just God's plan.

As we turn on the world news, and another black man shot dead is this trigger happy cop the one to blame. I can't believe this is the land from which we came. It seems like we are fighting this battle that nobody will win.

Let's reminisce on our parents past, where should I begin. As the world cries we've had enough, can we save the world on police brutality. Before someone else's child becomes another fatality.

Xscape

Release these shackles so I can finally be free. Too many bad memories of how our lives use to be. Go ahead, and let my daily struggles flow with the ink from my pen. So I thank Maya Angelou for teaching the world why caged birds sang. Yet our black youth are filled with ignorance, and too many materialistic thoughts, so what promises can this bring.

So how can we Xscape from hate and disgrace when our own country wants to judge by race. They tell us that these prison bars are our rightful place. Please tell me why our future is filled with bandanas and AK47s? I hope my son's greatest accomplishment is not the power of a gun. Maybe one day he will want to pick up a book for fun.

Many may pray that there is hope for our youth. Let these words I recite become nothing but the truth. Some say it might be a little too late. These shackles may hold me physically, but mentally I will always have the ability to Xscape.

Silence

Why keep me in silence? After all the lies, games, and blame, you still want to be in control. Your heart is all I want to hold, but mine you already stole. Can I have my chance to speak? Dominance is what you seek. I climbed many mountains just to have my chance as a woman to speak. No longer will I live my life in fear. Trust me with all this mental abuse; I feel the end is near.

Just because you are my man why does everything have to be your plan? Many nights when you slept, I prepared to take your life with your favorite custom made knife. When you were sleep you began to choke, even then I thought about slitting your throat.

The love I once had is no longer there; my heart is now consumed with hate. I need to be removed from this place, before I catch another legal case. Yes I said another, because it was my own step-brother who thought he could take my body for his own pleasure. Many cold nights I would run to the Legal System for help, there reply was what did you do to entertain his body parts.

All I could do is cry from all this sexual abuse. So once again I had to live this life in silence, but somehow I need to be brave. This is why I sent my step-brother to his early grave. My focus will no longer include you, from now on God will be the only man that will tell me what to do.

New Blood

Here I am God knees bowed wonder why my life is follow by this black cloud. You said all I have to do is to confess by tongue. It was your blood that you spilled when you were young. I no longer can do this all alone. One time in my life I didn't have a place to call home.

I can no longer walk around without the truth being told. Look at me now I am 41 years old. This world is so cold. Our youth is very bold. They are so lost. Do they know you paid the ultimate cost?

At times I feel scared. My life you spared. For the first time someone actually cared. You are the truth and the light. Now my favorite color is now white.

Many times I asked for my father's picture. Instead I will read this scripture. Psalms 27:3 is my favorite line. Yes I am the son of" Nine". Whatever his crime let me do his time. Why does my family focus on the past? That's what I ask.

Many nights I cried because as a child I been through so much. True I changed because of God's touch. What I want is to make this world united. Still Satan's all white jury wants me indicted. I still feel shackled like a runaway slave. I need to break these chains so I can be free. Finally, the world will get to see the real me.

I can honestly save I have no more pain. New heights I will gain. Yes I am the blame. I did play Satan's game, and won. Don't forget I still have a son. I tell him every day to say no to guns.

Our schools need more dedication, to lead this world in education. So before I go can we pray? Just to make it through this day. Don't forget to say one for my friend Ray. Right now he is still behind bars, with a lot of mental scars. Never give up, because of one mistake.

Some apologies may be late. Thought about Shawntae last night, gave her life after an unbelievable fight. Remember those crazy days on Hilltop; we had to stop because someone called the cops. Think about what we did was dumb, but at least we had fun.

Watch Me Burn

The sound of screams and shattered glass, maybe this makes you feel like a man because you are constantly beating my ass. My hand gets to shaking because my inner demons are starting to waking. Have you ever love someone so deep that you can't sleep at night. Now you're faced to relive last night from a big family fight.

    All you're trying to do is stay out of her sight, but now she got you feeling disgraced. All you can hear is nigga look at my face. Baby please don't leave, without you I can barely breathe. So go ahead and watch me burn, as my family tells me it's time to repent because I don't know my own strength. At times we say things we didn't really mean as it seems. We both need to control our tempers because when they blow it's like Hell on Earth, and our kids end up feeling cursed.

    As my lady walks the streets with a black eye, all she could do is cry from all this hurt and pain. He promised to never do it again, but it's you who suffers from his daily sins. On our final night another fight because I decided to leave from all this domestic abuse, no this is not another excuse. Take your hands off of me please because I can't breathe. With all the constant struggles, an unknown chemical is spilled.

All you can hear are his screams from spreading flames, deep down inside the world will say she is to blame. As I laid there gasping for air, my mind begins to wonder, because it was my temper that changed our world like thunder. My lady cried as I died, but there wasn't much to learn, as she stood there and watched me burn.

Autistic Thoughts

She stares at the moonlight as being showered by gloom. Deep down inside she is scared of the moon. My pretty baby, this world is so cold. I will never forget what your attacker did to you when you were only 7 years old. She prays to the heavens for a place that called peace. I watched from a distant as my daughter sleeps.

My baby is a motherless child in this world. Didn't even cry when she got the news her mother died. Family members called her coldhearted because she refused to cry for the deeply departed. Maybe they need to understand that she suffers from a mild form of autism.

All she needs in this world is God and me. I have had my own personal struggles, but my world is still my little girl. I chose to isolate my children from family, since their life choices are so unhealthy. Now that she is age 16, Danyel writes about so many traumatic things that she has seen.

After all the heartache she bared, many nights Danyel continues to ask why no one cared. Her constant negative feelings she had fought, but this is just another day in her autistic thoughts.

Dedicated to my daughter, Danyel L. Walker

11/23/2014

The Court Jester

How much longer shall I play the fool? So many hurtful things were said, which at the end of my life, wasn't too cool. So I am willing to play the game, but are you willing to pay ultimate price of fame. Because of life choices, our love seems to be surrounded by flames.

Too much heat to bear, my constant daily struggles, showed me you really didn't care. Maybe I am your fool; my heart was your stepping stool. So now my face stays painted in white, don't forget the black lonely tear drops. Since all your constant insults would never stop.

To the world you were there princess, but they treated me like public enemy number one. Maybe that's why you gave so many empty promises to my son. So how much longer should I be your fool, it's crazy how you all promises to have my back. Once you lost your power, maybe it's times to get your life on track.

Now the time has come to remove this mask, it's funny how times have changed since I chose my own class. As I walk down the streets of Enchanted Dreams, my world was once consumed with hate. How many more times should I be your fool? So many storms I had to weather, because now I finally got my life together.

Death Row

Here I am locked away like a cage animal. My only sense of life is surrounded by these pictures. Sooner or later they all will just fade away. I thought my love ones would be there for me, but boy was I mistaken.

My life is what the state has taken. For what, because I am black with a gun, the one person I thought cared, from a distance she just stared. I'm the one that made sure you were protected. Now I feel so neglected, my letters I sent you were all rejected.

It's sad that you don't have anyone. Do you think I can have just one picture of my son? Maybe you ignored me for fun. As I sit on death row waiting for them to call my number. Lord knows I will not be here come next summer.

To the world I am a criminal. Before you judge me get to know me, but that's not quite so simple. So by all means run to the media, and tell them the state will execute an innocent man. Maybe someone will understand.

If not, trust me all I can say is that I fought a good fight. My final words to my wife is that I have accepted Jesus Christ. As I try to hold back the tears, because I miss my peers. I have been dealing with these fears for years.

You know what is so sad all I ever wanted was a picture of my son. I figure this request would be easy since I took the charge for carrying her gun.

Chapter 5

Creative Hearts

Creative Hearts

What about my art of creativity. Could this be another story of nativity? Let me sins flow from the ink of this pen. Lord knows my life was crazy back then. My inspiration is still the *King of Pop*.

All I want is to strive for excellence, and never want to stop. Sometimes I write about pain and maybe pleasure. My stories are what the world gets to treasure. I have spent my whole life looking for peace. Kind of makes me wonder if it really exists.

So as I walk down this street called Dreams, I see many unrecognized faces of many races. Is this where I belong, maybe try singing your favorite song? When it starts to rain do we dance as my unborn child takes a glance? Can I even have another romance as we get close?

It was you that I chose. I hope this life is filled with appeal, because this place here is the real deal. Maybe it was all just a dream. I did have fun as it seems, can't wait to fall asleep because this place here plays for keeps.

The Falling Leaves

On a foggy early morning, we enjoyed the cool air. As we walked hand and hand many people would smile and glare. As the wind blew through her beautiful hair, I noticed the leaves were falling slowly. As my thoughts began to ponder, my phone began to ring who is this that could be calling.

As I answered the phone a familiar voice would start to speak. Wondering whose this distant voice from my past. Then a voice said I thought you remembered me why don't you seem to care. You put your love on sight so all I could do is stare.

The happiness that you have has increased my hatred. So many times you have played me like a fool? It's all good, the hurt and pain I have isn't really cool. I wonder if your women knew about all the games you played. Do you still promise them the world just so you can get laid?

I bet you still wonder who I am, many nights we made love uncontrollably. Now that I got your attention, seems like you and your new lady are living the good life I forgot to mention. You would tell me that two wrongs don't make a right.

I would do whatever it took just to keep you, even fight. All that ended last night. Your lady told me that you both kissed. I forgot to tell you she is my baby sister, which at times I would dismiss. Maybe you have an attraction for this family.

What you seem to forget, is now you are my new toy in this game of deceit. So you put on this show with your three piece suits, pretending that your life is so neat. Now you know that we play this game to win. So by all means take your last sip of gin.

Yes I said last, because from now on I am putting your life on blast. I will move like the coil of a snake. Trust me this family has a lot at stake. Your soul I would love to take. I hope your world crumbles like a huge earthquake.

The sight of you makes my blood boil. My sister tells me all the time how much she is in love with you. Her happiness will soon turn in to hurt, now isn't that funny. One thing about my sister is that she is a talker. I love playing this game even from your own personal stalker.

I was Lost, Now I'm Free

I believe in dreams again, maybe this feeling should never end. My talents are no longer locked away because I am free. If I should die this very day don't cry, because on earth we weren't meant to stay. I am confident that God will let me walk the streets of gold on Judgment Day. My tears of sadness will no longer flow like the Red Sea, I was lost, but now I am free.

In my life there was a lot of disappointments and pain, it was even hard for me to see the sunshine through the rain. So I was lost, but now I'm free, there is a change in me that the world can't really see. I felt so all alone, even at this very moment there is no true place to call my home. My faith in God has increased because of this secluded place called peace.

I watch my kids grow up with smiles, but laughter was never really my style. Each day I play the role of someone in control, but with headaches came another story untold. I was lost, but now I'm free. This just might be another daily plea filled with sin, but there are places we have dreamed of where some have never been.

So Father God I thank you for giving me this on chance to make a difference in someone's life. My faith is still strong, especially on that fateful day when you took my wife.

Let me be the one to lead, because my whole life has been surrounded by destruction and poverty. Close your eyes and reminisce of how I was lost, but now with faith from God I am free.

You've Gone Too Far

So many women have taken advantaged of my heart; some even ripped it completely apart. All I ever wanted was to show you how it feels to be loved. Maybe I should not have given you this new life, even wanted this romance to last more than just one night. I took you to the finest places, and even dined with many races.

What really hurts is how our relationship ended. You gone too far, never again will I ever have trust in you. I guess the rumors on the streets were true. I took you on trips around the world; even let you spend time with my little girl.

Many times she wanted a real mother, at the same time you gave your love to another. Did it really have to end this way? What more can I really say, but ask you to stay?

As I walk the street with my head held down, somehow I got to be strong. The whole world knew how you did me wrong, I refuse to sit here and write another sad song. My biggest down fall was becoming your charity case; maybe I should have treated you like yesterday's trash.

Friends tell me to focus more on God. Maybe I was being like a typical man that wanted every woman to understand. True my little girl's heart might be broken, but her faith is still with God.

At times I do feel bad; maybe this was my karma because so many hearts I broke just to get laid. Now I am on the opposite side of love stuck with this broken heart, so it seems the whole time I was getting played.

Confusion

I am lost in a world filled with confusion. My head is in the cloud with so much pollution. Many pretend their game is so air tight. In a sense it was all the same, which explain why you wasn't acting so right. Family shows you so many ill faces.

True some of us might not be 100 percent blood, but we all should still come together like hand in glove. My heart goes out to the" Blessed 7" Even though your mother is in heaven above. She is now resting with God, and his highest dove.

People say you should count your blessing well ok 5, 4, 3, 2, 1 God I am not selfish give the rest to my 11 year old son. I know the enemy is busy, which explains why he hides in the dark places. Just have faith in God and his light will shine in all spaces. Especially, now since my life seems to be surrounded by many legal cases.

Will my life ever have a sense of peace, maybe it is because of my love choices? True my heart still hurts; can I find a place that will inspire me to grow? How many more time can we accept the answer no? Is there a place where I can breathe positive air? For once in your life show the world that you care, and that your lives did not die in vain. Will this family recover, and live the America Dream, maybe we are all just living on hope as it seems.

This family may still be filled with confusion, but why follow them down the wrong path. It's time to make a change, focus more on healthy relationships with the Lord. Will he save our souls, before it is too late? I am living proof of what it is like to fall from grace. What I can honestly say for the first time in life is that I'm free from hate.

Written 04/11/2011

You are appreciated

So I decided to use a quote that was created by the Legendary Tupac. Guaranteed when all is said and done the world will be craving for more. Our black women, how many more times will she be your bitch or whore? I am not going to sit here, and act like I have never disrespected a black woman.

    So in my road of life I paid the ultimate cost for my actions. Now I focus on presenting a more positive reaction. So ladies you are appreciated, for giving birth to my one and only son. What matters to me the most, is your constant teaching method that maybe used because power is in the mind not who carries a gun. Ladies you are appreciated, can you forgive me for calling you a whore?

    When I was locked away because of injustice, it was your passion for the truth, which showed me you cared. I understand you had your constant struggles, and even ended up on welfare. In society you are treated like a constant fool even though our only attraction to a black woman is when she is our sex tool. So I wonder why our generation of boys disrespects them like used toys. Maybe all this disrespect began when we chose to walk out of your life, and refuse to give you the title of wife.

Ladies you are appreciated, it hurts my heart that some of my closes family and friends have been a victim to domestic violence. My last conversation was with a female friend, whose man would constantly dotted her eye. When she threatened to call the police he would begin to cry.

Last I checked love isn't supposed to hurt. How many times will he use that same lame excuse, for his own abuse? Many times J.W. prayed how all she wanted was to getaway. Even her little 14 years old brother wanted to help her find a way out of no way.

You are appreciated, so ladies after all you been through from the beginning of slavery to 2014 I am very appreciative for all your struggles so many of our women had to endure. How can we improve our own communities?

For starters as men we need to grab hold of our boys, and let them know that our women need to be cherished. Just imagine how life could be if we chose to focus more on the home life, and finally give our woman due process by giving them the title of wife.

Anyone but You

Seen everything disappear before my eyes, so many nights I cried. Remember the night I almost died. It's true we were in love very young. I want to do more than just have fun.

I don't want anyone but you. You told me there isn't much trust when it comes to men, maybe we can start things over. For the first time in my life I am sober. I really do care, my thoughts we can share, because of you my life has been spared.

When it comes to the streets let them talk. Just know that I don't want anyone but you. Don't sit here and cry, change your frown into a smile. After all you have been through; just know that I don't want anyone but you.

So many things we use to do. When the world chooses not to be bother and life's sin makes you "wanna holla". Just know this love is true I don't anyone but you.

Chapter 6

1ne Dream

Res ipsa loquitur (The thing itself speaks)

They say actions speak louder than words. Some of the things we did were kind of absurd. Granted we all suffer from some sort of pain, but as brothers why live like Able and Kane.

With all this pain, God took away the rain and replaced it with sunshine. My world is much better this time, no longer do I focus on anger. Family may throw stones, but that's alright I love the way it hurts.

No longer am I bound by your chains, but what I gained was my freedom. So your personal attacks have now faded to black. We do share a similar pain, but our angel now spread her wings in heaven. My heart does go out to you all, but your sense of negative drama is why I chose not to ever fall.

Beautiful Disaster

To the world I am a beautiful disaster. What more is society after? Her looks were stunning that many would kill to have. To the streets she was known as Lyric, with her poetic craft she could flow like the deep blue sea.

Her heart was fragile like glassware. Maybe her man really didn't care. His male child she would bare. The world would only stare at her beautiful black hair. Her mental scars told a story of abuse.

Mainly because of the road she would choose. She used her fake smile as her excuse. Her true thoughts would flow with her pen. Late nights she cried about her only true love that died. As he gets shot down with a gun all she had left was his only son.

Lovers and Friends

There was a time when I really needed that special person in my life. At home all alone for many nights, we would talk on the phone till the beak of dawn. When I felt my life was at risk, you prayed.

When times got tough, and I thought you would leave you stayed. At times I couldn't help, but to admire the love we have for each other. I guess this is why you would become my lover. Just the look in your eyes would capture my soul.

Our chemistry was as pure as gold. Spiritually we were in two different places. From our disagreements and differences we need our own spaces. No more lonely nights. I still at times wish I could hold you tight. Now I am living this single life. Just know for now everything will be alright.

Dedication

Maybe I should pray for the unloved, how about I ask the man above to show this world some love. We act more like runaway doves. True I can't recite one scripture. Show me a picture and I will speak the truth especially, to the young black youth.

There are those that use this for an excuse, maybe we should chase more waterfalls just in time to hear mama's call. I don't like the man in the mirror because I am afraid of his reflection.

Tell our nation's leaders that our kids need more education, and less segregation. As parents it is our job to give our children inspiration in order to receive this dedication.

Every night I still pray for protection, maybe Teirra gave me the answer when she wrote "The Breakthrough". I finally got my space as we fell from grace. Maybe now my enemies will be put in their place, to prevent me from catching a case.

Melissa told me we are in our last days so you better pray. True I miss them all at this time in my life, but when the things go who do I call? Much love for my blood because it runs deep in the streets. True I may get old; the devil could never own my soul.

Misunderstood

Grabbing my favorite black hood, it's crazy how quite these streets have been. As I begin my journey people would just stare at me as if I was about to sin. Something has changed I was no longer the talk of this small town. Matter of fact most people when they see me instead of smiles all I received was frowns.

What is it about me that changed? I no longer broke the rules or even hung out with the same crew. Then I heard 2 shots in the night, so there was no need to stick around so I flew. Am I dead to the world because of where I have been?

Maybe just maybe I am being judged because of my past, it is true I did a lot of people wrong back then. That was then; my focus is the future not the past. Sure life isn't quite what it used to be. Am I wrong for wanting a better life for my kids? I can't put all the focus on just one when I have three.

You know I see my enemies, but I fear my friends even my own girl wants to know where I been? Maybe I will just stimulate her mind if I could. Well I guess from now on to the world I am still misunderstood.

Written 06/15/2012

Peace

I refuse to live in a country whose main focus in violence. Maybe I am just a fool, but how many more lives do we have to lose. I try to stay in my own personal space, but why should we die because of our race? My brother tells me to just turn the other cheek, and we will have our world peace.

As I look in my rear view mirror of hope, let me ask you why you think I am so inferior. What hurts me is to see our people slaughtered on television for ratings. Didn't our leaders shed enough blood from a gunman's trigger, but my own brother can't even walk the streets of Baton Rouge unless he is called nigger.

I know the past has a bad habit of creeping up on us all, but who can we call for help when we fall. Our young black men, I worry about you so much because there is a war that we must fight, especially when you hang on the streets at night. All I am asking for is just a little peace, can we all get along. Why do you hate me?

The black community is so tired of going to funeral of our black men that has been murder by white trigger happy cops. This sense of violence has to stop. We can't walk away this time, because little Johnny is dead for a senseless crime. Maybe this is our sign of the times, but wait our president is black right? I don't mean to compromise executive orders, but our war is in these streets not the Mexican Borders.

I know some of you might not like what I'm saying, but it's my constitutional right. This piece of paper was create to keep us in chains, now the police walk away free after squeezing off rounds in our brains. What I refuse to do is fight violence with violence since my focus is no tolerance. It's 2015 and we need a resolution before someone gets an idea to start a revolution, just like Nat Turner.

Can we have a little peace? At least for one night in the streets, no more of our mother's crying tears. Her fears are that her son has died because he had nowhere to hide. One Friday night he stole somebody's ride, got caught by a cop who chose to enforce his own form of justice by squeezing several shots from his glock.

1ne Dream

1ne dream, everything is not what it seems. Life has never been the same since "God's Rain". Here let me explain. For many years my tears were always protected, and never neglected. My talent comes from the power of my pen, some stories about sin.

The rest are short versions of where I been. There were dark places of many races, traumatic court cases, and scarred faces. Mother cries because their babies died, somebody helplessly screamed why. Please don't run and hide, this time.

Hold up my name is Crime, and Crime doesn't pay, what about Baby Shay? They say just pray to make it from day to day, and God will make a way out of no way.

I now know why caged birds sang, did their vocals bring the American Dream. Rest in Peace Maya Angelou, one day we will celebrate with heavenly champagne. What more can we gain from all this pain?

I think Saundra is the blame, because she still weeps for her soldiers we lost in the streets. Her own son shot execution style from a police officer's gun, now isn't that deep. Nowadays everybody wants to play God, only he can decide who lives and who dies.

This is just a mere thought that runs through my head each night before I go to bed. Every breath we take is someone's violent death in another place. Every healthy smile tells us that hunger just struck another child. Can you feel the change, which is out of range?

I visualize this world being saved, for the sake of our children. As we sleep maybe there is a place called peace, which this whole nation tries to seek. Maybe one day we will not judge by color, and we can love one another like sister and brother. This is just reality as it seems like someone just dropped a tear, because of this 1ne dream.

Chapter 7

Masterpiece

Stranger in Moscow

I decided to make a change, because my old life had me going insane. My babies cried and called my name. Father God can you take away the pain. Tired of the world belittling me, can I have space why don't you let me be so my demons will finally set me free, my life was once consumed by rain. Happy tears will drown away the pain. As the locals look as if they want to hunt me down, am I a Stanger in Moscow.

My life has been flooded by your grace, as we prepare for Armageddon is Jerusalem such a place. Have you ever taken time to live or dream about some place you've never known? This is just a sense of my imagination, can you say you've actually been there before.

Until we conquer our inner fears, some may still haunt my own peers. My former life no longer has me bound. I am no longer a stranger in this small Tennessee town called Moscow.

Make That Change

Make that change, even though your old life is no longer the same. My focus is not longer trying to seek fortune and fame. Concentrate on making better choices, that God we have many voices. I have gone from being a homeless child with a dirty face, who constantly dreamed of a distant place. Maybe somewhere they all cared because my life was spared.

Make that change because the focus is not on you and me. Think about the hurt of a little child who constantly cries because of starvation. However, they are ignored because of this countries segregation. As I walk down the street called Skid Row, and seen so many people that were a lost cost.

We can save this world, which is filled with sorrow for a brighter tomorrow. Trust me our youth is so lost. We have too many leaders that are not true believers. I was always taught that one positive voice can change the world. So my focus is to change one person's life for the better.

As I close my eyes with discuss, and hear the laughs of those that walked by. Could it be really me pretending that they are not alone? So deep inside I just started to cry because now I have no place for my head to lie. So if this world is to make a change I decided to start with me. Maybe this bad dream will for once just let me be.

Masterpiece

As we mourn our loss knowing this feeling is just temporary. My veins still flow with pain of the past, what more can come of this I asked? True our winter storms will come and go, but can we really stand the rain.

Did all of our dreams end up being the same? At times I may still hurt, but I know longer feel cursed. So let me create this masterpiece. Many nights we talked about the streets of gold, is there such a place.

With many smiles, and a world that don't judge by race. I can honest say that I made a change, not because I talked with the *Man in the Mirror*, but God has remove malice from my heart. My older brother is getting old and his heart is still cold.

All we can do is pray for his soul. I can remember your teachings never feel inferior to man, but always follow God's plan. At times I may fall off track because of Satan's personal attacks.

So my sister Melissa as I envision God's masterpiece, maybe the world will see how I overcame obstacles. So my heart may feel weak as I cry because you are truly missed. God's tears from heaven did flow, so many of us didn't want you to go.

Yet our tears would still flow. So as your name is written in God's Hall of Fame it will forever be history, not a mystery. Now that my tears have dried, because I am still reminded that fateful day you died.

Dedicated to my sister Minister Melissa A. Williams (Missy)

October 11, 1958-March 23, 2012

Let Me Explain

Did our black youth refuse to accept the truth while Marvin sang" What's going on". Let me explain, sure we go fight wars, but why some of our baby mothers are called whores. Maybe because they ask their babies daddy's for help.

I think for once we should give women their rights and respect. There are those women that don't give a fuck if their child lives or dies, but what about the ones who struggle to make ends meet.

I know why caged birds sing; true Maya Angelou created this poem, but no matter what happens your mind will always be free. Let me explain, how come as black men we can't walk with a black hood.

I understand our youth might be thugged out, but watching our kids being shot down is what this is really about. I thank those who have read and supported my art from the beginning. Most of this started at the School of Lula Mae (my mother) I called my childhood a school, because my mother wanted us to learn so much in so little time.

Maybe that's why none of her 7 children went to prison for an infamous crime. I still hear M.J. "Man in the Mirror", but is society really trying to make a change or was his message just a little out of range. My life was like a shattered mirror, all broken in pieces.

If I told you the things I been through, your reply would be you must be joking. So my life changed when I wrote" The Breakthrough", however " My Struggles, My Faith" made life a little out of place. I told you about God hiding my tears from my peers, which you all" Let Me Explain" the true meaning of " God's Rain".

My Kids

You know I really love my kids, no matter how bad at times they can be. As a single father there were so many people that claimed they would be there for me. Just know my kids are my life, and I would go through Hell just to make sure they are safe.

For once the world will get a chance to know about the changes I been going through. My whole life is just like maze filled with so many different obstacles. The difference between then and now is that I put God first in my life. We all know that tomorrow is not promised to anyone.

I try to teach my son that power is in the mind not who carries a gun. At times Daniel Jr may think I am trying to discourage his dreams, but he needs to know that there is no "I" in team. I really do love my kids, my daughter Jaimie and I really didn't see eye to eye on so many issues.

There were a lot of things that could have been left unsaid; we cannot change the past because it's a brand new day. If I could give you any advice just spread your wings, and become a Black Butterfly. If you should ever fail just dust yourself off and give it one more try.

Can you all imagine how much I love my kids? My daughter Danyel, even though you have been judged by the world, and even had been called names by your peers. Just know that as your father I have dropped a tear. I have dropped a tear because I really do care.

Trust me we will go the extra mile because as your father I will never be scared. You are that one child that will carry on this dream continue to think positive, and create your own theme. Just know that I love you all. If the Lord shall call me home before I wake, I pray my soul he will take. After all as your father I do love you because you are my kids.

Dreams

As kids we gazed out the window on a lonely quiet night. Even when our lives wasn't so quite right. As young boy who played with his favorite Christmas toy. To a grown man that looked to the world for joy.

How can we find a place where dreams still come true? Close your eyes, make a wish, and thank your luck star. Your dreams will shine like the midnight star, no matter how close or far.

(Excerpts taken from an unfinished poem written 08-22-1994)

Daniel L. Walker, Sr

01-06-2015

The Beat of Happiness

Follow the beat of the happy drum; sing out loud so the world would want to come. In life I finally found a place called peace, it seems like the world refuse to let me be. A false prophet in my family claims that their everyday problems are my responsibility. My goal is to be recognized in God's Temple.

It's a blessing how "the Breakthrough" changed my life forever. When God cried each tear came from Heaven. My first disappointment happened at age 11. I decided to write "Concerned Feeling" it showed the world that my heart is still in the process of healing.

So now my life is surrounded by many positive smiles. Even though my family hasn't seen me in a while, but there are those who refuse to change their life styles. The beat of happiness, can you fill the vibration. Our mother's legacy continues to grow with another one of life's creations.

My life is no longer filled with many sad faces of the past what I asked was another task. As I climb the largest mountain to the highest peak it will be his greatness I will forever seek. I may now be free, but at times I may still follow that all familiar beat.

Window Pain

Here I am at the W Hotel on Peach Street near Midtown Atlanta. Only a very select few can begin to imagine how my lifestyle has changed. People begin to acknowledge how I am dressed to impress wearing my favorite Egyptian Cotton French Cuff shirt. I was about to have my first interview with the media about the success of my debut novel God's Rain, which has taken the world by storm.

As we both talked about how our life use to be, we began to reminisce those horrific events I use to see. As we both glanced at the streets below wondering what this world has to offer. She smiled and said from the look in your eyes I can tell you care. From her intriguing question, my feelings I began to share.

Growing up as a kid I thought my life was so unfair. So many stories of pain and struggle I began to bear. No matter how tough the road of life use to be, I am still optimistic about my future. Many nights I wondered if this plan would set me free. My life is like an open book, filled with so many untold stories.

Many nights I dreamed of being burnt in Hell. I use to hear those distant voices; maybe it was because of life's choices. So she asked what did I see when we gazed from my window pain? After all the opportunities that I am able to gain maybe now I can wish upon a star no matter how close or far.

As my interviewer was about to leave, she gave me a beautiful smile. I haven't seen one of those in a while. I know she replied, at times when you were sad I cried. God was always there, to care, to share, and to bare all of your pain. Before I leave, all God ever wanted was for the world to believe.

Can this be why your heart no longer grieves? God always protects his anointed; from that statement, ask yourself what would you do? As one of his highest angels, that's why God sent me to conduct this interview.

Dream Chaser

I'm getting closer to my dreams, at least is how it seems. My life has changed; no longer do I focus on women that are thirsty. As we get older there are those goals that may seem like they maybe unreachable. Some may fear failure, but for me I will just take it as another challenge.

All my life I have been a dream chaser, even though society's main focus is that green paper. To some people I just maybe a social media star, but my faith encourages me to go far. My hunger for success has been put to a test; however recognition of my own art is what I am after.

So no longer will I have tears, so change that sadness in to laughter. Some of you may feel intimidated, but life is a competition. Only the mentally strong will survive, which explains why so many unknown artists have committed career suicide.

After all is said and done, maybe my legacy can be passed down to my daughter or son. I used to live my life in shame, but now with all of my accomplishments the world will always remember my name.

30 Years

30 years, mostly filled with tears, because of untrustworthy peers. I remember Miss Stella's house, and things we did, to the world we were her kids. For me I needed a place to escape. Some place that was safe feared my home life was filled with hate.

So her home was my sense of peace. Now at age 13 my feeling was strong for so long. Tears would flow because I had to go. Two different roads young and old, my world was cold and bold. Who could I trust? My life was filled with daily sins from so called friends.

With this new life, then came a wife. Many tears from our kids every single night because of our fights, I had a lot to say with no voice. Life is about choices. My choice was to win or lose because of sin. Many nights I prayed for this hell to end.

I struggled for nights about redemption with my pen. Pray for me, my father please take time to pray for me. Can you just let me be? As I fight with my demons, maybe save my son from another one of life's rejections.

Here take this Bible for protection. Maybe I finally found peace because my life was lost. Being introduced to tragedy I did pay the ultimate cost. I felt suffocated by the world. Can you give me some room to breathe please?

As I fall to my knees, and ask for the Lord to come to my life. I believe you died for my sins. I tried to make it on my own, many nights I cried in this place called hell.

It's crazy how a single message can change your life forever. It took just one serious conversation to make sense. Her heart was burnt with loveless desire. I began to ask myself what I must do to cool off her hurt of displaced races.

So now 30 years later my pain is my past. What I gained was a second chance at another romance. As kids we played maybe Stella Cowart was our vessel to happiness. I thought I could avoid her belt. The road of life's wrath I felt.

So Alesia Perry you were her little girl. For me I was her little boy. Never really wanted to play with toys, I was so eager to look at life in his face. What I received was battle scars from this place.

So for 30 years I had tears that God's Rain tried to hide from my peers. We both heard our momma's cries. Maybe we both can give to the world what was taught to us. Despite what road we took at the end there was still love.

Simply Unbreakable

After all the struggles, and disappointments I am simply unbreakable. People can wish badly on me, but I will still make it. My life is in God's Hands, and his faith will help me understand. So now let us prepare for the next big battle because these scars of pain run deep. Don't ever make a mistake because I got what it takes there is no way, you fake false prophets will ever get to me. Why can't you see that God will not let this be because I am too much for you?

You can throw your stones, but all I ever wanted was to be left alone. The world knows that this sacred bond has been broken, yet I still hoping that these shackles have finally been released. It seems you're drowning in misery because I found a place called peace, and my world plays for keeps.

So go ahead Satan form your weapons because they will not prosper. In my darkest hour, it was there that God showed his power. After your given all I could take, I refuse to crumble since there was no way we would break. I found hope in my heart; just know that it would not fall apart.

There were times I wanted to give up, but God gave me encouragement to go on. As you see my son and daughter means the world to me, after all we been through we still are able to stand on our own two feet.

In my darkest hour my faith kept me alive, but at times I help my head up high. It feels compelling to tell this story since I am simply unbreakable. For years you have tried to stop me, but now since you're drowning in your pain and my new found fame show the world I have always been the leader in this game.

Even in defeat I will be strong, since my tears were held down for so long. I chose this poem to drain my tears, but after years of prayer my seclusion is nonexistence. So now I feel unbreakable because these manmade chains will no longer be able to hold me down.

Not Alone

A sleepless little child, can you find a place that has no pain. As his mother makes plans to move ahead, unsure of how much time is left. Her long journey across country is what she gained. She tries to run from her past, but all she ever wanted was forgiveness from her sinful past.

Many nights she cried in silence; just know you are not alone. You may feel pain, but not as great as his name. Our heavenly father will hold you, even when you don't know what to do. When all is lost and you paid the ultimate cost, you are not alone. You are not alone when your true love is thrown in jail, and your new residence is the Heartbreak Hotel.

Can you stop this hurting now, as your tear drops flow all across town. She has learned in life to treasure what you have, especially since there is no mom or dad. When it's quiet she finally cries in silence. Just for her child she smiles and laughs but you're faking. Deep down inside you don't know how you're going to make it.

You are not alone; we both may have stress, but just know that this is God's test. I thought these hard times were all mine, many nights I use to pray for fame. You may feel pain, but nothing is as great as his holy name.

Take your problems to the man above, because we may still feel pain what comes from above is showers of love that comes in his form of rain. His love will see you through just know that these words I quote are all true. What you just read came from my heart, because God's love will never fall apart. Just know you are not alone.

Let Go

Introduction: I use to think that maybe we weren't meant to be together. Maybe we should have focused more on us instead of trying to please society. What were we truly seeking? This question may never be answer, but your memory will carry on.

Poem: My close friends tell me it's time to let go. I understand your concern, but at times my heart still burns. Have you ever loved something or someone that had captured your soul? Lord can you truly hear me, maybe try casting a sign in the deep blue sky. I have a hard time accepting that my world is gone, but all I can do is to continue to hold on.

    Do you know what it feels like when all you had has died, I still remember that fated day, at times I still may cry? Even when I try to let go, you reappear in my dreams. It seems my life is a little out of touch, especially when you're hurting so much. Lord I need you right now, can you stop this rain from falling. I have drowned in my tears; it's your holy name that I am calling.

Well the time has come to let go, since I've lived with this pain. My feeling will never be the same. Life is about choices, and it was your decision to leave that fateful night. I was told that angels still sing, even when they have broken wings. So you gained your heavenly wings to soar high in the deep blue sky.

I don't have any regrets because you saved my life on so many occasions. Our legacy will forever be protected; all I want is for you to be acknowledged for your positivity. Remember that day you saved my life when I was going to end it all at Citiline Towers. When you died, I cried because you saved me in an attempt to commit suicide.

Fly Away (Excerpts from an unfinished poem)

Angels Fly Home, since they are never alone.

Never fear to drop a tear, for family or peers

Angels fly home, since there is no more room to roam.

On earth you had your time to stay; now it's time to fly away.

When I see you again

It hurts that you paid the ultimate cost, but trust me I will see you again. I guess time did catch up with us, since most of our lives we were gone like the wind. Some of the times I didn't really treat you right; however what I loved was your daily Bible scriptures you would recite.

Since you been gone there's been so much drama into my life. Many still question if I truly did love you as my wife. Sometimes I'm like a man on the run because they loved to kick my heart around for fun. Now I can see through their true colors, we weren't really sister and brothers.

Maybe my biggest mistake believes in the so called street code. Through the years when you needed a true friend, no one showed me that they really cared. When I see you again we will drink heavenly champagne, since on earth all we ever experienced was pain.

Through sadness came tears, maybe we didn't own the right because for years all that was left is my tears. As I stood knee deep in this river called pain, at times we pray for God to stop the rain from falling. When you left all I could do is brace for this early death. In time the world will see that my biggest crime was being naive by letting so many people play with my mind. When I see you again, we will talk about the times we shared. No one will ever know how much I cared.

At times many did question my loyalty, even though I treated you like royalty. We will see each other in due time, but what I gained is a worldwide audience and a piece of mind.

Free

Somehow I just need to be free. Memories of how life used to be at times my emotions begin to flow. No time for stress, just give all your worries to God, and watch them go away. True this life we have here is temporary; maybe at times my thoughts are like my choice of clothing, pure customary.

So let me ask you this question can I be me? For once I get to do what makes me happy. So let my encore play. I still love to wear my dark shades, not because I hide my eyes. Now that the rain has come and gone, did you know my tears have dried? So I just got to be free. My book cover was chosen because it represents me. I use to wear this mask; sad at one point in my life, but now I am happy.

Even with all my success at times I may still got hurt. Maybe my family wants me to think that I am still cursed. Can I be me? Can I truly be free? Free from all the pain, free from all the blame, I know my father's sins have left me in shame. Can I have some happiness again?

I refuse to let my final destination be Hell, true most of my nephew's life has been jail. Can I be free? Don't show fear because I get a chance to be me. A close family member (or so I thought) once told me not to come home expecting love with open arms.

That statement did hurt, but I know where I came from, and it was never home. I need a place that would keep me safe from harm. So I am finally free. Free from all this hate, disgrace, and negative things I use to constantly conquer me. My focus is trying to fulfill God's prophecy.

Daniel L. Walker Sr

In Loving Memory

Benny "9" Walker   Father

Lula M. Walker   Mother

Benny Walker Jr.   Brother

Melissa Williams   Sister

Teirra N. Walker   Wife

Afterword

Let me take this time to reflect on where I been in my life. It was by the grace of God that I have this opportunity to tell the world my story. For once let me completely be honest with you. I have told many stories of my struggles, disappointments, and pain.

I tell you these stories because I overcame them all, my mother died focusing on the past. What I promised myself is that I wouldn't let my past destroy the future. Let me tell you a quick story of a lady, who was a single parent of seven children.

This lady did her best to raise her children despite having very little education. She gave her life for her children. There was a time when she would walk in the snow with holes in her shoes just to make sure her children had clothes on their backs, and food on the table. That lady was our mother Lula M. Walker, and if it wasn't for her tough up bringing I wouldn't be the man that I am today.

Here I am in Atlanta, Georgia with my children, and looking at a homeless lady from across the street pushing a shopping cart. Instantly I thought about how that use to be me, but I was blessed enough to still have a roof over my head. In the early 90's I lived in a shelter for the homeless youth that had been abandoned by their families.

True I came from a large family, but I walked a different path then some of my mother's children. So here I was living in this shelter in Pittsburgh, Pennsylvania called Whale's Tales. Believe it or not as a teenager I learned so much living in this place.

Sometimes I think about some of the people that lived there with me. In 2000 I would be reunite with former roommates named Jonathan and Lauren. When they lived at Whale's Tales, both Jonathan and Lauren were the ideal couple, even our counselors would tell us many of us to try to be more like them.

So when we got reacquainted, you can tell by their body language that they let the road of life beat them down along with the problems of society. So with the success of my first novel God's Rain, all I ever wanted was to write something for the homeless children of the world.

I truly believe that God holds a special place in his heart for those who do not have a place to call home. So in 2014, we still have the issue of homelessness in America. I can honestly say I was once that homeless child that cried at night hoping this was just a bad dream. I still cry as an adult because the issue of homelessness has not gotten better, but much worst.

Acknowledgements

Over the years there have been so many people that have been in my corner, especially during out time of tragedy. So to everyone around the world that was affected by our story thank you for all of your love and support.

To my Lord and Savior Jesus Christ, thank you father for saving my life, and giving me another chance to save someone who is experiencing Hell on earth.

To **Carla Dunlap**- thank you for being such a positive influence in my life. You gave me so much great advice from a single parent's perspective, and inspired me to never give up.

To **Brittney Smith**- thank you for supporting this entire project, you were always in my corner even when some did not believe in me. To **Cassandra Brown**- thank you for your support, and I love you so much.

To **Ka'Lysta A. Greene**- I really don't know where to begin; we have such a great relationship. All I want is for you to continue to work hard, and believe in your dreams.

To **Alesia Perry**- I cannot begin to thank you for being there for me, and excepting my children in your life. I have made some very bad decisions in my life, but that was the past. What I love the most about you is how you never judged me on my past.

To ***Ka'Jan Perry***- You are only 3 years old, but you are so well advanced you have such a bright future. I am glad that I get to see you prosper into a positive young man.

To my children- ***Jaimie***, ***Danyel***, and ***Daniel Jr***, I wish your mother was here to share the success of our book. However, she played a huge role in my life, and was there when I struggled with writing. I love each one of you. ***Jaimie***- we had an up and down relationship, but all I want is for you to continue to be a great mother to your girls.

Danyel- you have experienced a lot of disappointments in your young life, but like I told you before without struggle there will be no progress. ***Daniel Jr***, - as I look in your eyes I see the hurt and pain of not having your mother in your life.

No matter who comes in your life, you will only have one mother. There is still a lot to learn in the road of life, but I am here to help you. I love you all.

Since the release of my first book God's Rain, I have received countless emails on how my book has changed someone's life. So to all my supporters' thank you so much, without you this experience would not be possible.

To **Charlia Boyer**- I can't thank you enough for all your hard work in bringing my story to life on my audio book. I really enjoyed working with you.

To my siblings- **Betty**, **Ann**, **David**, and **Terry** I love you all so much thanks for your support.

To **Marsha Wright**- Thank you for your support, it feels good to be acknowledged from someone from the United Kingdom.

To **Barbara D. Smith** and Family- First off I miss Los Angeles so much, and miss the great times we shared together. Melissa you have grown into a beautiful lady, and I have seen some of videos of you dancing. Barbara you have a star in the making.

Author Projects

Other Titles by the Author

God's Rain: Poetry of Love, Life, and Family (Release Date June 21, 2014)

Coming Soon

Words Unspoken (Coming 2015)

God's Rain: Poetry of Love, Life, and Family (Release Date July 10,2015)

Second Edition

Credits:

Walker, D., Walker, T., & Walker, D. (2014). Life. In *God's Rain: Poetry of Love, Life, and Family* (1st ed., Vol. 1, p. 94). Createspace.

Richie, J. (2009, January 19). Bus, car crash on Homestead Grays Bridge; 1 dead. *Bus, Car Crash on Homestead Grays Bridge; 1 Dead*

God's Rain Novel Becomes a Bestseller. (2014, September 30). Retrieved February 19, 2015, from http://www.briefingwire.com/pr/gods-rain-novel-becomes-a-bestseller

Company* Logo *Designed by Danyel L. Walker

www.ingramcontent.com/pod-product-compliance
Lightning Source LLC
Chambersburg PA
CBHW071124090426
42736CB00012B/1998